BOUNCING BACK FROM EXTINCTION

THE RETURN OF THE AMERICAN BISON

THERESA MORLOCK

PowerKiDS press.

New York

Published in 2018 by The Rosen Publishing Group, Inc.
29 East 21st Street, New York, NY 10010

First Edition

Editor: Theresa Morlock
Book Design: Reann Nye

Photo Credits: Cover Geoffrey Kuchera/Shutterstock.com; p. 4 BGSmith/Shutterstock.com; p. 5 (Pyrenean ibex) dragoms/Moment Open/Getty Images; p. 5 (jaguar) Travel Stock/ Shutterstock.com; p. 5 (Arctic fox, hippopotamus) bikeriderlondon/Shutterstock.com; pp. 5 (orangutan) Sergey Uryadnikov/Shutterstock.com; p. 5 (Wyoming toad) https://commons.wikimedia.org/wiki/ File:Bufo_baxteri-3.jpg; p. 6 Johan Swanepoel/Shutterstock.com; p. 7 Maria Jeffs/Shutterstock.com; p. 8 David Osborn/Shutterstock.com; p. 9 Tom Murphy/National Geographic/Getty Images; p. 10 eurobanks/Shutterstock.com; p. 11 Filip Fuxa/Shutterstock.com; p. 12 Warren Metcalf/ Shutterstock.com; pp. 13, 25 Thomas Fricke/Design Pics/First Light/Getty Images; p. 15 https:// en.wikipedia.org/wiki/File:Bison_skull_pile_edit.jpg; p. 16 Library of Congress/Corbis Historical/ Getty Images; p. 17 pingebat/Shutterstock.com; p. 19 Darren Baker/Shutterstock.com; p. 20 Dpolzin/ Shutterstock.com; pp. 21 Betty Shelton/Shutterstock.com; pp. 22, 23 Lee Prince/Shutterstock.com; p. 24 Marco Prati/Shutterstock.com; p. 27 Mayur Gala/Shutterstock.com; p. 28 Kris Wiktor/ Shutterstock.com; p. 29 Weldon Schloneger/Shutterstock.com; p. 30 Rambleon/Shutterstock.com.

Cataloging-in-Publication Data

Names: Morlock, Theresa.
Title: The return of the American bison / Theresa Morlock.
Description: New York : PowerKids Press, 2018. | Series: Bouncing back from extinction | Includes index.
Identifiers: ISBN 9781508156215 (pbk.) | ISBN 9781508156208 (library bound) | ISBN 9781508156086 (6 pack)
Subjects: LCSH: American bison–Juvenile literature.
Classification: LCC QL737.U53 M8417 2018 | DDC 599.64/3–dc23

Manufactured in the United States of America

CPSIA Compliance Information: Batch #BS17PK: For Further Information contact Rosen Publishing, New York, New York at 1-800-237-9932

CONTENTS

A TRAGIC PAST

For hundreds of years, the American bison freely roamed the plains of the United States. These mighty creatures were treated with respect by many Plains Indians, including the Sioux and Cheyenne, who depended on them to survive.

During the 1800s, white settlers began to change the landscape of the West. Settlers built railroads and towns, which limited bison **habitats**. The U.S. government encouraged hunters to target bison. Some people felt the great herds stood in the way of the country's progress.

Some settlers hunted bison for the **resources** they provided, such as fur, meat, and horns. Others hunted them for sport, killing many more than could be used. By the beginning of the 1900s, fewer than 1,000 bison were left in the wild.

Although they almost became extinct, thanks to many **conservation** efforts during the 20th century, bison are now considered a near threatened species.

CONSERVATION STATUS CHART

EXTINCT

Having no living members.

Pyrenean ibex

EXTINCT IN THE WILD

Living members only in captivity.

Wyoming toad

CRITICALLY ENDANGERED

At highest risk of becoming extinct.

Sumatran orangutan

ENDANGERED VULNERABLE

High risk of extinction in the wild.

hippopotamus

NEAR THREATENED

Likely to become endangered soon.

jaguar

LEAST CONCERN

Lowest risk of endangerment.

Arctic fox

BISON BASICS

To understand the history of the American bison, it's important to first know a little bit about the animal and its behaviors.

American bison are the largest land mammals in North America. They can weigh up to 2,200 pounds (998 kg) and stand 6 feet (1.8 m) tall. A bison's diet is made up of plains grasses, herbs, shrubs, and twigs.

BISON OR BUFFALO?

American bison are sometimes called buffalo. The American bison **species** is part of the family Bovidae. Asian buffalo, African buffalo, and cattle are also in the Bovidae family. Although the American bison species has some things in common with the Asian and African buffalo, American bison are not truly buffalo. They came to be called buffalo because early European explorers in America thought they looked like these animals. Today, many people still use either name to talk about this species.

African buffalo

A bison baby is called a calf. Calves are also sometimes called "red dogs" because of their orange-red color.

They spend most of their time roaming the land and **grazing**. Bison roam for great distances. They need lots of room in which to live.

Bison live in large herds. Females are called cows, and males are called bulls. A female bison is pregnant for nine months and gives birth once a year, during the spring. Bison only have one baby at a time.

Bison have special adaptations, which are changes that help them survive. They have poor eyesight but very good senses of smell and hearing. A bison's thick coat of fur makes it well adapted to life on the Great Plains, where the winters are very cold and snowy. Bisons' coats are so thick that snow doesn't melt on their backs.

In the wild, bison are hunted by wolves and a few other animals. Bison are very fast. They can run at speeds up to 40 miles (64.4 km) per hour. They also have sharp

A bison's lifespan in the wild ranges from 12 to 20 years.

horns that can grow up to 2 feet (0.6 m) long. They use these horns to protect themselves when attacked. Sadly, the bisons' adaptations didn't protect them from American settlers, who brought them to near extinction by limiting their habitats, hunting them for fur and meat, and killing entire herds.

IMPORTANCE TO PLAINS INDIANS

Bison were, and continue to be, important to the way of life of Plains Indians. Bison are a fundamental part of the religion and **culture** of Plains Indians. Many Plains Indians respect bison as a life-giving resource. In the days of the great bison herds, when Plains Indians killed a bison, they made sure not to waste any part of the bison's body. Bison provided meat, which was eaten both fresh and preserved. Tepees, clothes, soap, and tools were all made from bison body parts. Although the Plains Indians

American Indians used every part of a bison. Bladders were used to make water bags and bones were used to make arrowheads.

American Indian arrowheads

EUROPEAN ARRIVAL

When European settlers arrived in America, they changed the landscape, causing the bison population to suffer. Building farms divided up the lands that the bison had once roamed freely. The settlers also introduced **domesticated** cattle, which exposed bison to new diseases. The European settlers did not treat bison with the same respect that American Indians did. To them, bison were nothing more than an object to use and sell or a pest to get rid of.

hunted bison, they did so in a way that did not cause the bison's populations to drop dangerously low.

Many Plains Indian peoples felt that the bison was a powerful, sacred being. They valued the bison not only because it provided them with the tools to survive but also because it was a great creature. Many dances, prayers, and folktales celebrate the bison. Some groups of Plains Indians work to save the bison today.

THE FUR TRADE

With the arrival of European settlers came a rise in the fur trade. Bison were among the many animals that were hunted for their hides, or skin and fur. During the 18th and 19th centuries, people killed thousands of bison for the fur trade. Many American Indians hunted the bison to trade their hides for European goods and tools. Bison hides were very popular because they could be made

This American Indian girl is preparing a buffalo hide.

into warm robes and coats. Many U.S. soldiers wore bison coats during the winter.

The Hudson's Bay Company is a Canadian company that played a large part in the fur trade. In 1844, the Hudson's Bay Company reported that 75,000 bison robes were traded to posts in Canada. As time went on, people discovered better methods of cleaning hides, which increased the **demand** for them.

WESTWARD EXPANSION

During the early 1800s, the United States began to **expand** across the western half of the continent. White settlers traveled through the Great Plains, drawn by the promise of land and gold in the West. These settlers came into conflict with American Indians living on the Great Plains. Many felt that the American Indians stood in the way of progress.

Knowing how much the Plains Indians relied on bison to survive, settlers hunted bison in an effort to starve out Plains Indians and drive them from their traditional homelands. White setters killed immense numbers of bison to force out the Plains Indians, make way for railroads, and get money for their hides. Bison meat was used to feed railroad workers and army soldiers.

Some people collected bison bones to sell to companies that would crush them to make **fertilizer**. This photograph, which was taken during the 1870s, shows a pile of bison skulls waiting to be ground into fertilizer.

THE TRANSCONTINENTAL RAILROAD

The construction of the transcontinental railroad played a major part in the mass killing of bison. The railroad's construction began in 1863. When it was completed in 1869, people could travel coast to coast by rail for the first time.

Some people traveled west just to take part in bison hunts. Men shot bison from train windows as they passed herds. The railroads sold trips to "hunt by rail." Though fast and strong, the bison were no match for

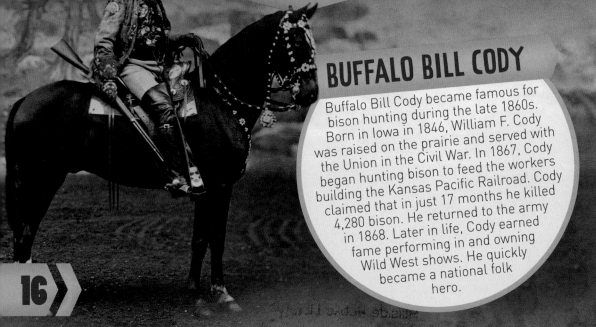

BUFFALO BILL CODY

Buffalo Bill Cody became famous for bison hunting during the late 1860s. Born in Iowa in 1846, William F. Cody was raised on the prairie and served with the Union in the Civil War. In 1867, Cody began hunting bison to feed the workers building the Kansas Pacific Railroad. Cody claimed that in just 17 months he killed 4,280 bison. He returned to the army in 1868. Later in life, Cody earned fame performing in and owning Wild West shows. He quickly became a national folk hero.

AMERICAN BISON
HABITAT

before 1850

after 1870

after 1880

Canada

United States

Mexico

As the West became more developed, bison habitats quickly shrank.

the hunters' guns. New developments in firearms made it possible to kill more bison than ever before. Hunter Orlando Brown killed nearly 6,000 bison himself.

THE END OF THE SOUTHERN HERD

The railroad divided the Great Plains bison into two herds: a northern herd and a southern herd. The railroad also made it easier to ship bison hides and meat, which increased the demand. In 1865, hunters killed 1 million bison. By 1871, the number of bison killed totaled 5 million. Between 1871 and 1875, the southern herd was completely wiped out.

Laws protecting bison were often too weak or too late to be helpful. For example, in 1864, the Idaho state government passed a bison protection law, but by that time Idaho's bison had already been wiped out. After the extinction of the southern herd, the population of the northern herd continued to drop. When there were fewer than 1,000 bison left in the United States, the first real efforts to conserve the species began.

THE BISON PROTECTION BILL OF 1874

In 1874, Congress passed a bill to protect bison. The bill made it illegal for any non-American Indian to kill or harm a female bison. It also tried to curb wastefulness by stating that a person could only kill as many male bison as they were able to use or sell for food. This bill addressed the concern that bison were being killed needlessly. Unfortunately, President Ulysses S. Grant didn't sign the bill into law.

During the 1870s, some people began to capture bison for private herds. These bison were often raised for their meat.

EFFECTS OF EXTERMINATION

Bison are very important members of their **ecosystem**. By stomping the soil with their hooves and by wallowing, or rolling around in the dirt, bison open up space for seeds to settle and grow. They keep grasslands healthy by grazing as they move. Without bison, grasses can cover too much soil and choke out other plant growth, such as wildflowers. Bison also contribute to their ecosystem by leaving behind waste, which fertilizes the soil. When bison began to disappear from the plains, the ecosystem suffered.

Bison wallow to cool off in hot weather. The patches of earth they stir up are good for the ecosystem.

Apart from being a key part of the ecosystem, bisons' lives are valuable in their own right. Bison have lived in North America for thousands of years, much longer than the American settlers who almost brought about their extinction.

EFFORTS TO RESTORE BISON

During the late 1800s, people began to speak out more about conservation. The government established the first national parks including Yellowstone National Park in 1872. Congress passed the first federal law concerned with protecting the American bison in 1894. This law punished anyone who killed bison with a $1,000 fine or prison time.

THE YELLOWSTONE BISON

Since prehistoric times, herds of bison have lived in the area that's now Yellowstone National Park. During the early 1900s, efforts to protect the bison in Yellowstone played a large part in their recovery throughout the United States. In 1902, there were only 24 bison left in Yellowstone. Today, there are 5,500. The Yellowstone herd is one of the few pure wild bison herds in the United States. Other herds have mixed with cattle.

Theodore Roosevelt was very important to the conservation movement. During his presidency, he worked to pass many laws to protect the environment and suffering species.

In 1905, Theodore Roosevelt, William Hornaday, and other conservationists created the American Bison Society. The society's goal was to rescue the bison from extinction. They tried to achieve this by relocating herds to wildlife **refuges** where they would be protected from hunters. In 1907, the society shipped 15 bison from the Bronx Zoo to the Wichita Mountains Wildlife Refuge in Oklahoma. In 1908, the U.S. government established the National Bison Range in Montana as a refuge for bison.

During the early 1900s, as bison were moved to protected parks and refuges, their populations slowly recovered from the losses suffered during the mid- to late 1800s. As these protected herds grew, some of the members were relocated to new areas to mix with existing herds and expand their numbers. By 1910, the number of bison in North America had grown to about 2,100. By 1919, the population was about 12,500. By 1935, the

The ITBC is made up of members of 58 American Indian tribes from 19 states. Members work together to educate the public about bison, organize bison transportation, and help create healthy bison herds.

bison recovery was so successful that the American Bison Society was no longer needed.

American Indians played a huge role in bison recovery. In 1990, the Inter Tribal Bison Council, or ITBC, was formed. This council is made up of members of many tribes, all of whom have the goal of returning bison to American Indian territories. There are over 15,000 bison in the ITBC herd.

SETTING AN EXAMPLE

During the late 1800s, few federal policies existed to protect wildlife. Although some laws later limited bison hunting, the effort that truly rescued bison from extinction was the creation of national parks. These parks and refuges created habitats in which the bison populations could recover naturally. Conservationist leaders such as Theodore Roosevelt began to popularize the idea of preserving natural habitats, which had been treated with little respect during the land expansion of the 1800s.

The near loss of bison taught many people that wildlife could not be treated so carelessly. The bison recovery programs and protection policies set an example for how other at-risk species should be treated in the United States in the future.

In 1973, President Richard Nixon signed the Endangered Species Act to protect at-risk species from extinction. Bison were protected under this act.

People have often thought of bison as a symbol of the spirit of the West. On May 9, 2016, President Barack Obama signed the National Bison **Legacy** Act, making the American bison the official national mammal of the United States.

The bison's successful recovery from the edge of extinction is exciting for many reasons. It shows that, by working together and being more aware of our effect

If we continue to be aware of how our actions affect wildlife such as American bison, their populations should continue to be healthy.

on the environment, we can save the species that have been harmed by human activities.

However, the work isn't over yet. Although bison populations are growing, their habitats are not. National parks must be protected and expanded to make sure that bison have the space and resources they need to survive. The first step to conserving Earth's wonderful species is valuing their lives and their habitats.

HISTORY OF THE AMERICAN BISON

1700s–1800s Europeans settle in North America, changing bison habitats and bringing cattle, which spread disease to bison.

Westward expansion begins, driving American Indians out of the Great Plains and further limiting bison habitats. Mass hunting of bison begins in the 1830s. **early 1800s**

1871–1875 The southern herd is wiped out.

Congress passes a bill to limit bison hunting, but President Grant refuses to sign it into law. **1874**

1894 A federal law makes bison hunting illegal.

The American Bison Society is established. **1905**

1907 Fifteen bison are sent from the Bronx Zoo to the Wichita Mountains Wildlife Refuge in Oklahoma.

The National Bison Range is established in Montana as a refuge for bison. **1908**

1973 The Endangered Species Act is passed.

The Inter Tribal Bison Council is formed. **1990**

2016 Barack Obama signs the National Bison Legacy Act.

GLOSSARY

conservation: Efforts to care for the natural world.

culture: The beliefs and ways of life of a certain group of people.

demand: A strong request for something.

domesticated: Bred and raised for use by people.

ecosystem: A natural community of living and nonliving things.

expand: To spread out or grow larger.

fertilizer: Something added to the soil to help plants grow.

graze: To feed on grass.

habitat: The natural home for plants, animals, and other living things.

legacy: The lasting effect of a person or thing.

refuge: A place that provides shelter or protection.

resources: Things that occur in nature and can be used as supplies or sources of energy.

species: A group of plants or animals that are all the same kind.

INDEX

WEBSITES

Due to the changing nature of Internet links, PowerKids Press has developed an
online list of websites related to the subject of this book. This site is updated regularly.
Please use this link to access the list: www.powerkidslinks.com/bbe/bison